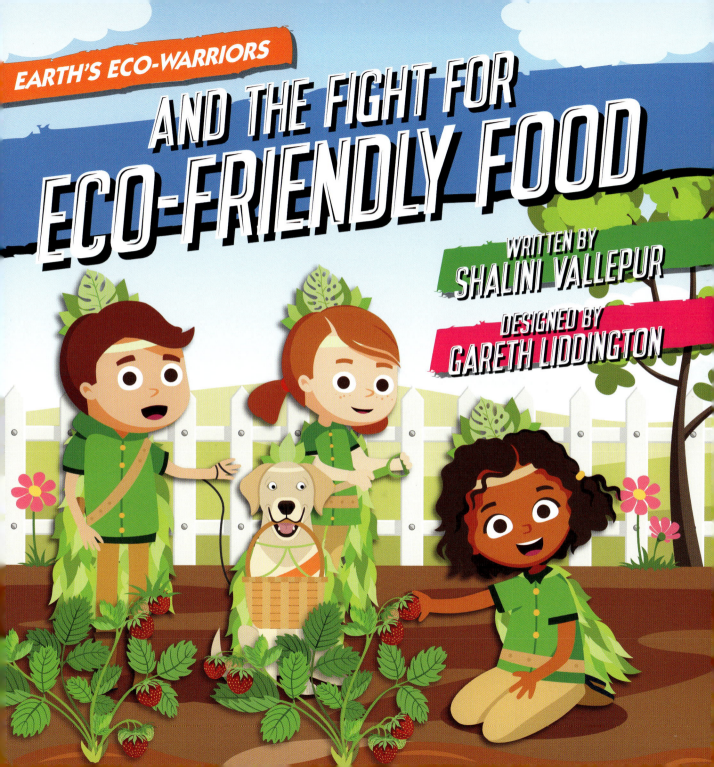

The Planet Promise
I promise to:

Rethink what I use and buy.
Refuse what I don't need.
Reduce my waste and carbon footprint.
Reuse things when I can.
Recycle as much as I can.
Rot food in a compost bin.
Repair broken things.

Earth's Eco-Warriors are fighting for eco-friendly food. But what is eco-friendly food, and why should we fight for it? Eco-friendly food is food that is sustainable and doesn't damage or harm the environment. Do you know where the food you eat comes from and how it gets to the supermarket? Some foods are grown or transported in a way that can damage the environment. We must rethink what food we buy and think about ways that we can make food eco-friendly.

www.littlebluehousebooks.com

Copyright © 2025 by Little Blue House, Mendota Heights, MN 55120. All rights reserved. No part of this book may be reproduced or utilized in any form or by any means without written permission from the publisher.

Little Blue House is distributed by North Star Editions: sales@northstareditions.com | 888-417-0195

Library of Congress Control Number: 2024936737

ISBN
979-8-89359-001-2 (hardcover)
979-8-89359-011-1 (paperback)
979-8-89359-031-9 (ebook pdf)
979-8-89359-021-0 (hosted ebook)

Printed in the United States of America
Mankato, MN
082024

Eco-words that look like this are explained on page 24.

WE ARE EARTH'S ECO-WARRIORS

Are you an Eco-Warrior? Greta, Bailey, and Pietro are Earth's Eco-Warriors! Eco-Warriors care about the environment. They made the Planet Promise and are trying to save planet Earth.

WHAT'S IN SEASON?

Let's make a food calendar! You can use the food calendar to keep track of what foods are in season. This will help to make your food miles lower and reduce pollution in the environment!

THINGS YOU WILL NEED

- Ruler
- Colored pens and pencils
- Piece of poster board

ASK AN ADULT TO HELP YOU FIND OUT WHEN DIFFERENT FOODS ARE IN SEASON NEAR YOU.

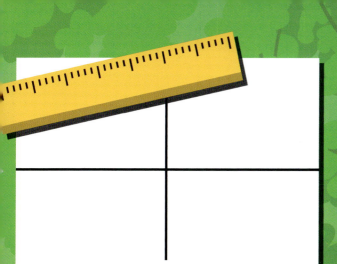

1. Using the ruler and a pen, draw lines on the poster board to make four sections.

2. Write one season in each section.

4. Draw your favorite fruits and vegetables in the appropriate seasons.

3. Ask an adult to help you find out what grows locally in each season where you live.

ECO-WORDS

compost bin	A special bin where yard waste and some food scraps turn into soil.
energy	A type of power, such as light or heat, that can be used to do something.
environment	The natural world.
food miles	A measurement that tracks how much energy is used in transporting food.
fuel	Something that can be used to make energy or to power something.
harvested	When fully grown crops have been picked.
local	Found, grown, or made in a place that is nearby.
nutrients	Natural things that plants and animals need in order to grow and stay healthy.
pollution	Harmful or poisonous things being added to an environment.
produce	Plants that have been grown to be eaten, such as vegetables.
rot	When something breaks down and decays.
sustainable	Done in a way that doesn't harm the environment or use up Earth's natural resources.
transported	Carried something from one place to another.

INDEX

compost, 2, 13–15, 21
environment, 2–3, 6, 21–22
farmers, 7–9
food miles, 4–5, 9–10, 22
Planet Promise, 2–3, 11, 13
plastic, 4, 10–11
pollution, 6, 22
produce, 8–10
recycling, 2, 12, 15
waste, 2, 11–12, 15–16, 18–19
zero-waste, 10

PHOTO CREDITS

Cover & Throughout – Olga1818, Gabi Wolf, Kazakova Maryia, Fancy Tapis, Tarikdiz, Inspiring, 2&3 – CandyDuck, 4&5 – DRogatnev, jujuk swandono, Vexturo, 6&7 – seeyah panwan, Incomible, Inspiring, Spreadthesign, 8&9 – ONYXprj, GoodStudio, Iconic Bestiary, 10&11 – ecco, 14&15 – Laia Design Lab, Eloku, Maquiladora, NotionPic, Park Ji Sun, Lorelyn Medina, Kaimen, 16&17 – Alfmaler, AQmari, rok77, Oceloti, Sunshine Vector, 18&19 – MicroOne, Elegant Solution, 20&21 – Visual Generation, Iryna Alex, 22&23 – Oleksii Arseniuk, karakotsya, Rvector, OLEG525, Andrii Bezvershenko, tsventina_ivanova, uiliaaa.

Images are courtesy of Shutterstock.com. With thanks to Getty Images, Thinkstock Photo, and iStockphoto.

All facts, statistics, web addresses, and URLs in this book were verified as valid and accurate at the time of writing. No responsibility for any changes to external websites or references can be accepted by either the author or the publisher.